SOMEONE I LOVE DIED
Published by David C Cook
4050 Lee Vance View
Colorado Springs, CO 80918 U.S.A.

David C Cook Distribution Canada
55 Woodslee Avenue, Paris, Ontario, Canada N3L 3E5

David C Cook U.K., Kingsway Communications
Eastbourne, East Sussex BN23 6NT, England

The graphic circle C logo is a registered trademark of David C Cook.

All Scripture quotations are taken from the Holy Bible, New International Version®,
NIV®. Copyright © 1973, 1978, 1984 by Biblica, Inc™. Used by permission
of Zondervan. All rights reserved worldwide. www.zondervan.com.

LCCN 2011941023
ISBN 978-1-4347-0291-3
eISBN 978-1-4347-0394-1

Text © 2012 Christine Harder Tangvald
First edition published by Chariot Books © 1988 Christine
Harder Tangvald, ISBN 1-55513-490-4

The Team for Revision: Susan Tjaden, Caitlyn York
Cover Design: Amy Konyndyk
Cover Illustrations: Anne Kennedy

Reviewed for best practices in helping children deal with trauma by Janet McCormack, D. Min.,
B.C.C. and Heather Davediuk Gingrich, Ph.D., both from Denver Seminary, Colorado USA.
Some interactive components provided by Mary Grace Becker

Manufactured in Shen Zhen, Guang Dong, P.R. China, in November 2011 by Printplus Limited.
Third Edition 2012

1 2 3 4 5 6 7 8 9 10

101711

Someone
I Love
Died

Christine Harder Tangvald

Illustrated by Anne Kennedy

With praise to Jesus and glory to God,
I dedicate this book to:
My wonderful parents, Harry and Frankie Harder,
And to my beloved son, Thor Roald Tangvald

They have already crossed the chasm and are
experiencing the reality of eternal life.
Wait for me. Wait for me.

Christine Harder Tangvald

For Nanas everywhere, and those
who love them

Anne Kennedy

Someone I know who died is _____.
I liked _____ a lot.

Here is a picture of _____.

Draw a picture or attach a photograph.
You can do this now or later.

When a person dies, some people think that is the end of everything.
But they are *wrong*, aren't they?
That's not how God works at all.

You see, God has a plan for everything …
A plan for *life*.
A plan for *death*.
And a plan for *life after death*.

But thinking about death can be sort of sad and upsetting, can't it?

*Draw how your face looks when you are
thinking about the person who died.*

And there are lots of things about death that are hard to understand.

To help us understand a little bit better, let's start at the very beginning.

Did you know that a long time ago, God created the body for the very first man out of the dust of the earth?

He did.

God created people special—different from the animals. He made people a lot like Himself—in His own image (Genesis 1:27).

And God breathed into the man's body the *breath of life*, and man became a *living soul* (Genesis 2:7).

When one of God's people dies, God moves the breath of life back *out* of the body to a special place we call Heaven, a place we can't see right now.

It's true!

A very important part of the person does not die … *ever!*

This is the part we call the *soul*—the part that lived inside the body … the part that makes us laugh and cry and listen and feel and pray and think.

This part of the person has moved to Heaven to live with Jesus forever and ever and ever.

And not only that, but ...

Guess who *likes* it in Heaven?
Guess who *loves* it in Heaven?
_____ does!

Because Heaven is a place filled with *joy* (Matthew 5:12).

So when a person dies, the body is like an empty house.
Nobody lives in there anymore.

Since it isn't needed anymore, we put the body in a large box called a
casket, or in a special vase called an urn. Then, very carefully, we bury
the casket in the ground. But it's okay, because *the soul moved out* and is
already happy in Heaven.

Even though we can't see the soul with our eyes, we know this is true because God told us so in the Bible.

Understanding this is hard, but it's all a part of God's plan.

Is there anything you are wondering about right now?

For the person who died, it is the end of life here on earth, but it is the beginning of life in Heaven.

It's sort of like the person has a new BIRTHDAY in Heaven—a new beginning! And just like our birthdays here are very happy days for us, their birthdays in Heaven are very happy days too.

But do you feel happy when someone dies? _____.

If the person in Heaven is happy, then why aren't *we* happy?

It doesn't seem fair. We wish the person who died could come back and stay here with us. But that can't happen. It just can't.
So we are lonely, and we feel really *upset*.
It's okay to feel upset. In fact, it's okay to feel any way you feel.

Some people feel sad or angry.
Some people don't.
Some people feel lonely or scared.
Some people don't.

And some people don't know exactly how they feel, except that they
are really upset.

However you feel is okay. You might want to cry and cry. Sometimes it
feels good to cry. Crying is another way to say, "I love you."

How do you feel right now? _____

Draw a picture showing how you feel.

But you will feel better again after a while. You will be happy again.
Maybe you don't think so right now, but it will happen.

You won't feel so lonely. And you won't be so sad. You'll start to smile
again … and then even laugh.

You might even play and _____ and
_____!

Maybe not right now, but later.

You will!

Sometimes talking about things can make you feel better. Maybe you want to tell someone how you feel *right now!*

Who can you talk to when you're upset?

You can talk to Mom and Dad, to your friends, to your pastor, or to _____ and _____.

But it's especially good to talk to God when we are upset. After all, God understands. He knows we don't want someone we love to die.

Sometimes we need to talk to God even if we don't really want to. We can tell God *exactly* how we feel right now.

Sometimes when we talk to God, it gives us a calm, quiet feeling inside called *peace*. We feel safer and stronger when we trust God.

What is something you are sad or upset about?

_____

What would you like to ask God?

_____

What do you want to tell God?

_____

People can die when they are young or when they are old or at any age in between. It's not their fault when they die. And it is not *your* fault when someone dies.

Do you wonder why people die?

Sometimes it is because of being really sick with a disease.
Sometimes it is because of an accident.
Sometimes it is because of old age.
And sometimes it is other things.

What did the person you know die from?

_____

Do you wonder how people get to go to Heaven?

Oh, this is the *best* part of God's plan. *Jesus* is the One who opens the door to Heaven. And Jesus invites everyone in.

You see, God sent His own Son, Jesus, to be our Savior:

Jesus lived here on earth.
      Jesus died here on earth.
            But God raised Jesus right *up* from being dead.

It's true! It was a miracle! Now Jesus lives in Heaven.

When we accept Jesus as our personal friend and Savior, *all* our sins are forgiven, and He opens the door for us to Heaven.

And *everyone* is invited!

_____ is invited too.

"By grace you have been saved, through faith" (Ephesians 2:8).

Jesus said, "I am the resurrection and the life. He who believes in me will live, even though he dies; and whoever lives and believes in me will never die. Do you believe this?" (John 11:25–26).

Is Jesus your personal friend and Savior? _____.

Thank You, Jesus, for opening the door to Heaven for me and for
_____ (Ephesians 2:8; Isaiah 61:10—62:3).

Do you know how fast a person's soul goes to Heaven?

Faster than you can clap your hands!
     Faster than you can stomp your feet!
       Faster than you can say your name!

That is how fast the soul goes to Heaven when a person dies.

Jesus told one man, "Today you will be with me in paradise" (Luke 23:43).
Today means *right away*.

Do you wonder *where* Heaven is and *what* it is like?
Do you wonder if there are stars in Heaven?
How about flowers and trees and animals and sunshine?

Does it rain in Heaven?
Will there be rainbows?

I hope so, don't you? But we really don't know. We don't know exactly
where Heaven is or what it is like. But we don't have to know, because
God knows.

But we do know Heaven is wonderful. It is not a sad or scary place to be. It is a happy place, a fun place, a terrific place. In fact, Heaven is better than the very best place you can think of.

Jesus said so. He said, "In my Father's house are many rooms…. I am going there to prepare a place for you" (John 14:2).

And, we can trust Jesus' promise because Jesus never, ever lies. Never! *Ever!*

Oh, yes! Heaven is one of the best parts of God's plan.

What do you think Heaven is like?

_____

And guess who is already there! *Lots* of people are already in Heaven. You probably know some of them.

Who of your friends and family are already in Heaven?

_____

_____

_____

And lots of people from the Bible are already in Heaven, like:

Noah, Moses, and Jonah,
King David,
Matthew, Mark, Luke, and John,
Mary and Martha

Who else can you name?

_____

And aren't there *angels* in Heaven? There certainly are. Lots of them.

I wonder how many people are already in Heaven?

I wonder what they are doing *right now?*

Draw a picture here of what you think Heaven might be like.

Aren't you glad God has a plan? A plan of *hope* and *joy*.

Here are some things I now know:

- It is not my fault if someone dies.

- It is okay to feel however I feel.

- The person who died is just fine. The soul moved out of the body to a special place we call Heaven.

- Jesus opens the door to Heaven, and *everyone* is invited in.

- Heaven is not a sad or scary place. Heaven is wonderful … a place of joy. Jesus said so.

- God will help me through sad, hard times, and sometime later I will feel happy again.

- Someday, all God's people will meet with Jesus in Heaven. That will be a happy, happy day.

Thank You, God, for Your plan!

"For God so loved the world that he gave his one and only Son, that whoever believes in him shall not perish but have eternal life" (John 3:16).

What are you glad about? _____

Prayer

Dear God,

Hi, it's me, _____.

Thank You for Your plan, God. Thank You for life here on earth and for life in Heaven.

Thank You for making Heaven safe and happy so I don't have to worry.

God, I want to feel safe and happy too. Please help me when I'm sad. Help me when I'm lonely or mad. And help me if I get upset.

I'm so glad to know I will feel better again after a while.

Thank You, Jesus, for being my very own friend and Savior. Thank You for opening the door to Heaven. You are the most important part of God's plan ... and mine!

Knowing about this makes me feel better. Lots better. But if I have more questions and mixed-up feelings, I will be talking to You again, God.

Really soon.

AMEN

Suggestions for Parents

1. Include the Child in Family Mourning

Give children something valuable—your time and attention. Include them in family mourning so they don't feel left out. They need to have a feeling of belonging in times of sorrow as well as in times of joy.

2. Talk It Out

Encourage children to talk openly about how they feel. Listen to what they are really saying. Use phrases such as "I wonder …" or "One question I have is …" or "I feel …" to open the lines of communication to such topics as anger, guilt, fear, etc. Death often makes us feel helpless and vulnerable. Talking out our feelings is an excellent therapy.

Be sure to use a normal tone of voice. Avoid whispering or using an unnatural voice.

3. Respect Each Child's Feelings

Permit children to participate, but don't force them to. Please do not be judgmental if they do not act or respond as you think they should. Some children may even seem distant.

Allow each child to vent any or all of the emotions that are associated with the grieving process: shock, denial, anger, frustration, sadness, fear, guilt, despair, panic, etc.

Do not discourage children from crying. Likewise, do not encourage them to display unfelt emotions. Let them feel how they feel.

4. Give Physical Reassurance

Physical reassurance is essential. Hug children, hold hands, tuck them in at night, etc. Also make frequent, positive eye contact. Wink, or just nod your head with a slight smile. These methods of comfort can be as important as anything you might say. Physical reassurance alleviates the fear of being abandoned.

5. Prepare the Child for Future Events

Don't surprise children with unpleasant experiences. Explain step by step the procedures for what is going to happen now. Explain some important terms, including some positive terms: casket, viewing the body, funeral, cemetery, cremation, grave, soul, Heaven, God, Jesus, etc.

Don't assume children know what is happening.

6. Give Honest Answers

Answer each child's questions honestly, but don't go into more detail than is needed or can be understood.

Gently explain the immediate cause of death—accident, old age, illness. Children want to know too. Also, this diffuses the feeling that somehow they caused the death. Assure them that nothing they have said or wished or done has contributed to the person's death in any way. And assure children that this is not about to happen to them.

7. Provide Escape Time

Give the child opportunities to interact with other children and times to escape the constant feelings of sadness that can surround a death.

8. Accept Support from Others

Accept support for both yourself and your children—from family, from friends, from your church, and from God.

Allow others the opportunity to show their love and care for you by letting them help and support you through this difficult time.

9. Pray Together

Our security is in the Lord. In the midst of your sorrow, stand on the solid rock of God's Word. Use the security of Jesus' promise as an anchor—for yourself and for your children.

Join hands with family and friends, including the children, and pray—whatever is on your heart.

God hears. And God understands. He really does.

My wish is that this book might provide a tangible tool of comfort, security, and help for children and adults as you face a difficult loss.
Jesus loves you.
I love you.

Christine Harder Tangvald